Augustine and the Journey to Wholeness

Robert Innes

Vicar of Belmont, Durham Diocese

GROVE BOOKS LIMITED
RIDLEY HALL RD CAMBRIDGE CB3 9HU

Contents

The Cover Illustration shows the conversion of St Augustine, which occurred through him hearing a child's voice singing in a garden in Milan: 'take up and read.' The picture is one of 17 scenes created by Benozzo Gozzoli in 1465 and which adorn the choir of the church of St Augustine in the Italian hilltown of San Gimignano.

First Impression February 2004
ISSN 0262-799X
ISBN 1 85174 556 4

Introduction

1

Why This Booklet?

We live in an age in which there is a massive interest in how people can find increased satisfaction, self-esteem, meaning and fulfilment. There is a widespread quest for some sort of personal psychological or spiritual 'wholeness.' Both in the world and in the church, people routinely look to various kinds of therapeutic counselling to help them address these questions. The demand for counselling is vast. Some 5,000 accredited counsellors and therapists, charging from £10 to more than £80 per hour, make their living from meeting this huge demand.[1] According to one estimate, half a million people now work full and part-time as counsellors.[2]

> *There is a widespread quest for some sort of personal psychological or spiritual 'wholeness'*

Alongside the growth of counselling there is a loss of confidence in the traditional resources of the church for meeting spiritual and psychological needs. I witnessed this first-hand when I was a theological college tutor. In their pastoral assignments, ordinands all too often handed in work which owed everything to the popular psychologists and almost nothing to the gospel. Of course, it was invariably a Christianized version of psychology—with an assortment of biblical texts used to add a religious sheen. This is not to say that modern psychological insights and practice do not have their place! But candidates really struggled to work out how the insights they had learnt in their Bible or doctrine classes had any 'cash value' in pastoral practice.

So the aim of this booklet (as with some other booklets in this series) is to try to make accessible some of the rich spiritual resources from the Christian tradition in the hope that they might connect with contemporary spiritual and psychological need.

Why Augustine?

But why Augustine? (And we are talking here about the great 4th–5th century St Augustine of Hippo,[3] not the 7th century St Augustine of Canterbury.)

Isn't Augustine the dusty old fellow who was hopelessly hung up on sin and sex, and is better quietly forgotten? Well here are four good reasons to take a serious look at Augustine:

- Whether or not we like Augustine, we cannot escape him! Augustine stands at the root of basic aspects of modern subjectivity, not least our fascination with the inner workings of our minds and souls.[4]

- Much specifically Western Christian spirituality is indebted to Augustine. The 12th century mystics Bernard and Richard of St Victor were both Augustinian Canons, later medieval mystics such as St Teresa and the author of the *Cloud of Unknowing* were deeply influenced by Augustine, and Martin Luther was an Augustinian monk.[5]

- For all that it is popularly ridiculed, Augustine's analysis of human sin and desire is remarkably incisive. For this reason he has sometimes been called 'the first psychologist.' The great theologian Wolfhart Pannenberg rightly comments that many modern treatments of sin have been unsuccessful because they have over hastily dismissed Augustine's teaching.[6]

- Where Augustine gets it wrong, we must try to understand the nature and extent of his errors, so that we do not inadvertently throw the Christian baby out with the cultural bathwater.

What This Booklet is About

The following sections of the booklet try to explain Augustine's 'spiritual psychology.' They are rooted in his fundamental idea of 'desire,' and they try to show how the mind can attain to wholeness by the proper ordering and fulfilment of desire. Next, I discuss three areas of Augustine's thought where he is frequently both written-off and misunderstood, namely his views on the body, sex and women. Then I give what seems to me a contemporary application of Augustinian spirituality—the ethos and methods of the Alcoholics Anonymous programme. Finally, I give a few signposts to help any who are interested in journeying further in the company of this great saint.

Augustine's Sociable Spirituality 2

People sometimes think that 'spirituality' is about the lonely quest of the soul for God.

And a selective reading of Augustine might support this. In reality, however, friendship was crucially important for Augustine. Before he became a Christian, he liked nothing better than to discuss philosophy with a group of male friends. After his conversion, Augustine came to see the monastic life as the best means of living under God. So, in 388 he set up a small community along with his friends, in which all property was held in common. Then, in 395 when he became a bishop, he set up a monastery for clerics in his bishop's house at Hippo, for which he wrote a monastic rule.

Carolinne White, in her work on patristic views of friendship, comments: 'With Augustine we reach the culmination of fourth-century Christian theories of friendship, for it is he who provides the most profound views, touching on many areas of Christian life and doctrine and according a crucial role to friendship in each Christian's progress towards salvation.'[7] Augustine held that by loving a friend we see the love which is the bond between two friends, and that love is none other than God the Holy Spirit. So in loving the love between friends we love God.[8]

So in loving the love between friends we love God

His interest in self-examination was linked to his interest in community building not opposed to it

The strongly social context to Augustine's thought is extremely important, and offers a thought-provoking critique of contemporary Western spirituality. Actually, Augustine lived with a level of sociability that few of us could tolerate. However close our friends we might baulk at sharing all our clothes with them! Nonetheless, if Augustine were able to visit a typical British church today, he would surely point out that our lack of spiritual depth was directly related to our shallow community life. And when we turn to look at Augustine's 'psychology,' it is important to realize that his interest in self-examination was linked to his interest in building community, not opposed to it.

3 Augustine and the Desire of God

At the heart of Augustine's psychology is what he calls 'desire,' a word which is synonymous in his vocabulary with 'love' and with 'will.'

Augustine's analysis of the mind speaks to us today, because he takes so seriously passion and emotion in forming our sense of self. By contrast, Greek classical thought (and also post-Enlightenment thought) had an unrealistically high view of reason. The philosophers thought that a good and happy life could readily be obtained by the virtuous control of the mind over the passions and the body. Augustine had proved in his own experience that this did not work. He knew himself to be moved by desire, and he had discovered that he could not motivate himself to do good without the refashioning of his basic desires.[9]

Augustine's mental life and his spirituality, was therefore—as it is for most of us—a struggle between competing patterns of desire. We might long for the sense of wholeness that we find in abandoning ourselves to God—the experience of being 'lost in wonder, love and praise.' But the reality, most of the time, is that our love of God is in tension with a host of other yearnings.[10]

Perhaps the most important spiritual development in Augustine's own life was his rejection of Manichean (and Gnostic) beliefs. The Manichees divided the human person into a good and spiritual self held in a potentially evil body. For them, spiritual progress meant freeing the spiritual from the bodily. In their scheme, it was possible to assign sinful desires to a body which is 'not really my true self.'

This kind of Gnostic 'splitting' has represented perhaps the most serious and constant threat to proper Christian spirituality throughout the ages. It enables people to justify to themselves doing one thing with their bodies and another thing with their minds. I think of a colleague who has been charged with a sexual offence against an under-age girl, with disastrous consequences for his family and his parish. It is a perpetual risk to those who are 'professionally religious' that we will 'split' a religious self from (say) a bodily and sexual self.

Augustine set his face firmly against the Manichees.[11] He knew a host of competing desires within his own soul and he accepted that all of these desires were part of his true self. Wholeness, the integration of the self, would come from ordering all these desires within a single pattern of desire and love for God. This meant a continuous struggle between the spirit and the flesh requiring constant vigilance and checking of evil desires. It was a project not just for mystics and monks but for everyone. As he says: 'The whole life of a good Christian is a holy desire.'[12]

Our Natural State of Sickness

For Augustine, the great mass of humanity lives in a state of radical fallenness. Fallen humanity is characterized by a neglect of its basic orientation towards God.

People live in the mistaken belief that fulfilment of desires for material and fleshly things would be sufficient to bring them happiness. Augustine gives an important autobiographical statement of this mistake in a description of his youth. He says:

> I came to Carthage, where a cauldron of illicit loves leapt and boiled about me. I was not yet in love, but I was in love with love, and from the depth of my need hated myself for not more keenly feeling the need...For within I was hungry, yet [though I was hungry for the want of it] I did not hunger for it: I had no desire whatever for incorruptible food, not because I had it in abundance but the emptier I was the more I hated the thought of it. Because of all this my soul was sick...[13]

This is a typically deep piece of writing. On the surface, it is an account of the 17-year-old Augustine arriving in a big city and feeling an intense desire to love and be loved. But at a second, symbolic, level the account introduces the leading psychological theme of desire which has gone astray. In granting free reign to carnal desires, human beings experience a state of self-division: hungry/not hungry, loving/hating. At this level, it is not Augustine but 'everyman' who is the subject. And for the philosophically inclined, there is also a third level, at which Augustine hints at Neo-Platonic beliefs concerning the fragmentation of the soul which turns away from God and loses itself in physical objects.[14]

It is within the will, at the level of 'desire,' that the most devastating evidence of humanity's sickness is revealed. Augustine distinguishes two kinds of affliction of the will. The first, and most straightforward, is the voluntary willing of something wrong. Adam eating the forbidden apple, or Augustine's own youthful theft of pears are examples. In such cases, Adam's successors lack a sufficiently motivating knowledge of their own highest good, so that they choose something which is less than the best, or sinful.

The second, and psychologically more subtle affliction of the will, is characterized by a person finding himself divided against himself in carrying out what he knows to be good. He does what he does not will and does not do what he wills (Romans 7). Augustine describes with great insight the process whereby voluntary sin leads to the involuntary sin of a divided will.

> The consequence of a distorted will is passion. By servitude to passion, habit is formed, and habit to which there is no resistance becomes necessity. By these links, as it were, connected to one another (hence my term chain), a harsh bondage held me under restraint.[15]

A person who allows an unchecked desire for some unworthy object to take root in her mind soon discovers that her mind is held in the grip of habit. Sin brings about its own punishment in fostering, through habit, the compulsion to sin. What began as a 'voluntary' sin becomes an involuntary addiction to sin. The person finds that even when she knows the good, she is unable to do it. She has lost that freedom which is constituted by her knowledge, will and feeling being wholeheartedly united in the object of her desire. She is a slave to sin.

Sin brings about its own punishment in fostering, through habit, the compulsion to sin

Augustine realized that sin is pleasurable—'naughty but nice'—that is why we are attracted to it. But like the White Witch's Turkish Delight in Lewis's *The Lion, the Witch and the Wardrobe*, sinful objects are addictive: the more you get, the more you want. In the end they just leave you feeling sick. The tragedy is that once the sinner acquires a taste for sin, he or she loses the desire for more wholesome food. And that, says Augustine, is the plight of humanity: we have lost the will to seek and do good and are all, in various ways and degrees, addicted to sinful desires and behaviour patterns.

Uncovering the Desire of God 4

Fallen humanity, as Augustine describes it, presents a sorry picture. Turning away from God, who alone satisfies our soul, the person suffers from a 'restless heart,'[16] and we may imagine the restlessness of a patient suffering from some terminal fever.

The disease is indeed fatal for many. But for some, those who can read the signs, the symptoms themselves provide a clue to the remedy.

'I can't get no satisfaction, though I try, and I try and I try,' is a line from a modern song, but it could equally be the keynote to Augustine's view of the fallen self. The inability of the soul to find satisfaction from material or fleshly sources of pleasure, is a kind of negative sign of the soul's true desire for God. The state of restlessness spurs the person on in search of that which will truly satisfy. In fact the failure of so many, indeed of *all* material objects to satisfy, pushes the heart in the direction of spiritual goods. Each material good becomes a sign pointing away from itself to the One who can truly satisfy.[17]

Using Platonic terms (for Augustine was schooled in Platonic philosophy before he turned to the study of Scripture), Augustine describes his own ascent towards God. Unsatisfied by material pleasures he turned inward from the desires of the body to the life of the soul. He ascended from the lower part of the soul, that region which deals with sense-perception and imagination, through the soul's power of judging temporal things, to the highest part of the soul which deals with the contemplation of eternal truths.[18] At length, Augustine received a momentary, mystical experience of God.

This Platonic language of 'ascent' has deeply influenced Christian spirituality. But Augustine is not speaking here of anything specifically Christian. What he refers to is what we would call 'spiritual experience.' We might compare a modern person whose experience of a beautiful sunset or a superb concert convinces them that there 'must be more to life than all this.'

Augustine found he lacked the spiritual strength to remain in this mystical state. His 'weakness' reasserted itself, and he tumbled back down to the material realm. But he was a changed man. For he now carried with him, as a trace in his memory, an experience which he took to be truly satisfying. The desire for God had been aroused. 'I returned to my old habits, bearing nothing with me but a memory of delight, and a desire as for something of which I had caught the fragrance but which I had not yet the strength to eat.'[19]

Sustaining the Mystical Vision

Augustine's reflections on the weakness of the human will in attaining and sustaining the mystical vision of God led him to a striking re-assessment of the nature of human motivation. He concluded that a person cannot move himself to action merely through his own will-power, nor can he autonomously respond to what is given by his intellect. Rather, a person can act only if they can mobilize their feelings, only if they are 'affected' by an external object of delight. 'When the right action and the true aim has begun to appear clearly, unless it also be delighted in and loved, there is no doing, no devotion, no good life. Even after his duty and his proper aim shall begin to become known to him, unless he also take delight in and feel a love for it, he neither does his duty, nor sets about it, nor lives rightly.'[20] *Delight*, concluded Augustine, is the only possible source of action, nothing else can move the will.

However, God did not make himself available as an object of delight, in the same tangible way that Augustine was accustomed to delight in the beauty of an African sunset or the embrace of his concubine. And so, Augustine came to realize that the processes that enable a person to take delight in God are not only hidden from them, but are actually unconscious and beyond their control. 'The fact that those things which make for our successful progress towards God should cause us delight is not acquired by our own intentions, earnestness and the value of our own good will—but is dependent on the inspiration granted us by God.'[21]

Augustine is adama[n]t that we cannot pull ourselves up by our own bootstraps

Augustine's reflections on the interplay between the will and sources of motivation which lie beyond the will's control are among his most suggestive interpretations of the human condition. Theologically, they underpin his insistence against all comers that we are saved by grace, not by our human endeavour. Augustine is adamant that we cannot pull ourselves up by our own bootstraps; all we contribute to our own salvation is our sin! Psychologically, his observations anticipate some of the much later exploration of the unconscious offered by Sigmund Freud. Where Freud's ego is limited in its freedom of action by the response of the unconscious to sources of pleasure, Augustine's self is chained in sin until the right 'chemistry' of delight and desire arises within it.

Strengthening the Desire for God   5

The appetite for God having been awakened, it must be fostered and strengthened.

And so Augustine urges his readers, in many different images, to desire God more intently. A recurring model in his commentary on the Psalms is the legendary Idithun, who 'leaps beyond' earthly things towards the vision of God. At three key points in his major theological work *de Trinitate*, Augustine quotes Psalm 105.3–4: 'Seek his face always.'[22] The life of someone on the path to spiritual healing is charged with yearning and longing. Augustine's model of the self is one of tension, movement, and change—closer in some ways to the self conjured for us by modern psychoanalysis than the control of emotion and detachment from pleasure and pain that was the ideal of the ancient Stoic.

Augustine talks of the movement towards God as an 'extension' of the soul. And he contrasts this with the 'distension' of a life which is scattered amongst numerous temporal and sensible desires. He suggests that the person who loves the world is like someone who immerses himself in the river of temporal things and allows himself to be swept along by it. The person who loves God, on the other hand, clings fast to the tree, which is Christ, planted by the river.[23] The desire of God both extends and consolidates the self, whilst desire for the world tends to overwhelm and fragment it.

Augustine's notion of 'strengthening' or 'extending' desire has two senses. Firstly, he refers to the extension of the mind through godly desire. The image Augustine uses here is of stretching the opening of a sack to make it capable of holding more. 'For just as, if you would fill a bag, and knowing how big the thing is that shall be given, you stretch the opening of the sack or skin…so God by deferring our hope stretches our desire; by the desiring stretches the mind; by stretching makes it more capacious.'[24]

Secondly, Augustine refers to the strengthening of desire itself. The picture here is the familiar Pauline one of the athlete straining to attain the prize. 'Holy longing' is like exercise; the more of it you do, the more of it you are capable.

These two forms of strengthening are bound together. When someone extends her own spiritual capacity through desiring God, she finds that her desire is strengthened. And in desiring more, she further extends the capacity of her soul. Thus a virtuous circle operates linking the desire of God with the growth of the self. We might say that someone becomes a 'bigger person' through growth in her relationship with God.

In summary, the desire for God is at work in both a negative and a positive manner to transform the self. In its negative aspect, the desire of God engenders that restlessness which drives us to ascend from the physical to the spiritual. In its positive aspect, the desire of God brings that pleasure which incites our further desire and enjoyment of God. In the first case we are talking about the lack of a desired object (the 'God-shaped hole at the centre of every human heart,' as the *Emmaus* course puts it); in the second case we are speaking about further enjoyment of the God in whom our hearts have already begun to find their fulfilment.

6 The Desire of God Fulfilled

The recovery of the divine image in human beings is likened by Augustine to the recovery of a person from illness or injury.

The first stage of the cure is to remove the cause of the debility. One must throw off the fever or remove the missile stuck in the body. This corresponds to Christian conversion, the turning around of the person from a preoccupation with the world to a Godward orientation, and the claiming of forgiveness of sins through the gracious work of Christ. But then there is the long, slow work of recovering from the weakness left by the fever or the wound left by the missile. This is a matter of continual formation, 'of daily advances whereby the soul is made new.'[25]

In *de Trinitate*, Augustine shows how transformation works itself out in the highest part of the mind, in what we might call 'the true self.' This is a matter of the human self being remade in the image of the triune God. Human beings discern the divine image in their remembering, understanding and loving of themselves. However, in fallen humanity these functions have been injured. The fallen self has lost the ability to see and love itself accurately and truthfully. This capacity cannot be regained from within the self's own resources. Rather, to regain true relations with itself, the mind must look beyond itself to God who is the source of truth and love. Through an increased understanding and loving of God, the self may increasingly see itself as God sees it, and so learn how to value and love itself properly.

On the Last Day, a person will see God face to face. The mind will then know what it is to remember, understand and love in perfect accordance with God's own knowledge. This state will correspond to the perfection of the divine image in humanity, that is, the self's accurate and truthful remembering, understanding and loving of itself. 'We shall be like him because we shall see him as he is.' And we shall, consequently, see ourselves as we truly are.

The long and slow positive transformation of the mind corresponds to the progressive degradation of the body through ageing.[26] This might have tempted the earlier and more strongly Platonist Augustine to regard the body as a bit of a hindrance to the formation of the self. But the mature Augustine of de Trinitate rightly insists that, insofar as a person is conformed to the image of the divine Son,[27] he shares in the death and resurrection of the body.[28] The person who has kept faith in Christ, who has continued to make steady progress in inner renewal, will get back his body at the end of the world, 'not for punishment but for glory.'[29] The present mortal body will be transformed into a strong, incorruptible and glorious body.[30]

The mature Augustine took a distinctively positive view of the passions. Here he disagreed strongly with the Stoics. Augustine could not recommend the Stoic moral principle of apatheia—which he took to mean 'the state in which the mind cannot be touched by any emotion.' Of such a life, he scathingly says: 'who would not judge this insensitivity to be the worst of all moral defects?'[31] Where the Stoics took the passions to be a kind of intellectual sickness, Augustine takes them to be expressions of the will. So evil resides not in the passions themselves but in the faulty orientation of the will.

The mature Augustine took a distinctively positive view of the passions

Peter Brown aptly reflects Augustine's 'high' view of the emotions in his comment that for Augustine 'the life of feeling was what really counted in personal growth.'[32] The person who has attained a relatively high level of growth will be one who *desires* eternal life, *fears* sins and temptation, feels *gladness* in good works and experiences *grief* in his own shortcomings and failings.[33] So in *City of God* (chapter 14) Augustine lists a whole range of emotions with examples of how they are to be approved inasmuch as they spring from the basic attitude of love of God. Here Augustine's thought anticipates some modern insights that suggest 'emotional intelligence' is at the heart of personal growth.[34]

Augustine is realistic in his view that there are some basic differences between the kind of 'emotional wholeness' that can be achieved on this earth and that to be experienced in the world to come. In the latter there will be nothing to cause grief or pain, and these emotions will cease. But in this world grief and pain may reflect praiseworthy charity towards our fellow human beings. So Augustine caustically remarks: 'Complete exemption from pain, whilst we are in this place of misery, is…a piece of luck that one has to pay a high price for; the price of inhumanity of mind and insensitivity of body.'[35] The morally praiseworthy person will exhibit not just those emotions which are to be found in heaven, but also those which are symptoms of the brokenness of the world. Here Augustine may be contrasted with some contemporary humanistic psychology, where the darker human emotions seem to find little place in the life of the healed individual.

Augustine thus describes the resurrection life as one in which the desire of the mind is fulfilled in eternal contemplation of God, the desire of the body is fulfilled in incorruptibility, and the emotions are each experienced in appropriate ways. This will be a state of supreme order, with the soul ordered under God and the body ordered under the soul. God is accorded the supreme rank, the self and other human souls are ranked equally below God, whilst the body and external material goods are ordered under the soul. The person is made perfectly whole.

Augustine thus concludes his *de Trinitate,* a work of huge mental imagination and effort, with a beautiful and heartfelt prayer:

> I have sought you and desired to see intellectually what I have believed, and I have argued and toiled much. O Lord my God, my one hope, listen to me lest out of weariness I stop wanting to seek you, but let me seek your face always, and with ardour. Do you yourself give me the strength to seek, having caused yourself to be found and having given me the hope of finding you more and more. Before you lies my strength and my weakness; preserve the one, heal the other. Before you lies my knowledge and my ignorance; where you have opened to me, receive me as I come in; where you have shut to me, open to me as I knock. Let me remember you, let me understand you, let me love you. Increase these things in me until you restore me to wholeness [*ad integrum*].

Some Areas of Difficulty in Augustine's Spirituality

7

1. His Suspicion of Bodily Pleasure

Whilst the fulfilment of the desire of God seems to entail the fulfilment of all the person's other legitimate desires, Augustine has a less than full-blooded commitment to fulfilling the desires of the body. Undoubtedly his notion of 'ordering' the body does grant the body real value. In his mature writing he is far from the active dislike of the body preached by the Manichees, and has moved beyond the austere tolerance of the body characteristic of Neo-Platonism. One could not say of the later Augustine, as Porphyry said of Plotinus, that he 'seemed ashamed of being in the body'![36] Yet John Burnaby rightly comments that, whilst he could sometimes maintain a more liberal view as a teacher, Augustine had, for himself, 'a profound distrust of all natural pleasures which he was little concerned to disguise.'[37]

In this respect, Augustine was a child of his time: affected by the negative view of the body conveyed in the Stoicism of his day, as well as deeply influenced by the Genesis account of The Fall. Augustine's distrust of bodily pleasure certainly cast its long shadow over subsequent Western spirituality, and is something which undoubtedly has to be corrected in our own age.

Thus the theological instincts of the liturgists were right (even if their prose was ugly) when they revised the prayer which appears in Anglican Common Worship as the Collect for the Sixth Sunday after Trinity:

> Merciful God, you have prepared for those who love you such good things as pass our understanding. Pour into our hearts such love towards you, that we, loving you in all things *and above all things*, may obtain your promises...

The Platonic spiritual path was a matter of loving God *rather* than loving the material world. Today's materialist, by contrast, loves the material realm and forgets about God. The truly Christian way is both to love the Creator and to allow that love to inform and condition our love for the material realm. We do not so much transfer our affections from the physical to the spiritual, as allow the love of God to transform us so that our love of earthly things is given its proper place.

2. His Views on Sex

Perhaps more important for us today than Augustine's uneasiness with physical pleasure are his views on sex. In our day, we tend to assume that spirituality and sexuality are closely linked. Both spirituality and sexuality touch the core of our selves, and we suppose that someone who has problems in one department is quite likely to exhibit symptoms in the other. If Augustine is wrong about sex we might suppose him to be wrong about spirituality as well.

Now at the outset two things need to be made clear. First, our attitudes to sex are strongly socially conditioned. For example, the question of 'what turns you on' depends on cultural symbol systems and varies from one culture to another. Secondly, if Augustine had a 'low' view of sex, it was not because he thought it was 'dirty,' but because he suspected it of being 'irrational.' To see how this could form a natural part of his thought world (whilst it does not form part of ours), we need to look at his context.

The Roman Social Context

'The past is another country; they do things differently there.' In no matter is this truer than in patristic attitudes to sexuality and celibacy. And one of the best accounts of this, to us strange, world is given by Peter Brown in his book *The Body and Society*.[38]

Brown describes a Roman society that was terribly exposed to suffering and death. Life expectancy in the patristic era was under 25 years. Five children were required from each family just to keep the population constant. In such a situation, reproduction became a social duty, maintained by civic habit even when not directly encouraged by the imperial taxation rules. The continuation of Roman society required a strong ideology of marriage and procreation. In such a context, celibacy became an act of social protest and an affirmation of Christian freedom from the social and familial orders of the imperial world.

In such a context, celibacy became a act of social prote:

Upper-class Roman attitudes to women and sexuality were characterized by what Brown describes as 'male puritanism.' Roman aristocrats looked down on barbarians, slaves and women from a position of unchallenged dominance. Women were understood, from a biological perspective, as failed males. It followed that the Roman male must exercise careful self-discipline over his body to avoid the development of 'womanish' traits, such as irrational anger or over-indulgence in food or sex. Brown concludes that Roman attitudes were characterized by a '*severitas*, a hard-bitten, manly austerity that made few concessions to women or pleasure.' He finds 'little support for the widespread Romantic notion that the pre-Christian Roman world was a sunny Eden of the unrepressed.'[39]

The Roman sexual ethic primarily reflected the need to maintain social order. Only sexually significant acts were of note. A man might have intercourse with female slaves without comment, and the sexual activity or exploitation of lower class women was a matter of indifference to the law.

Augustine's Sexual History

Augustine's own sexual history reflects this social context. In brief: Augustine was born in 354 in the little north African town of Thagaste. In his teens, he left home for the big city of Carthage. At the age of 17, and to his mother Monica's regret, he took to his bed a girl of low social standing, whose name he does not disclose. A year later Augustine became a Manichee 'auditor.' Unwilling entirely to renounce the pleasures of the flesh and become one of Mani's 'elect,' the young Augustine famously prayed, 'Lord give me chastity but not yet.'[40] Augustine kept his concubine for 15 years. Early on in their relationship, she bore him one son, the unwanted and ironically named, but then deeply loved Adeodatus ('gift of God'). Augustine's knowledge of natural methods of contraception prevented the birth of further children.

Meanwhile, Augustine's career as a teacher took him from Carthage on to Rome and then to Milan. He was soon recognized as a gifted orator and writer and had prospects of securing a senior position in government. But his career was frustrated by lack of funds. A good dowry from a rich wife would open the right doors. Marriage to his lower class partner was out of the question on grounds of convention and law, not to mention finance. And so, Monica arranged for Augustine's marriage to a suitable Milanese bride.

The prospect of marriage precipitated what seems to modern readers one of the most outrageous events in Augustine's life—the dismissal of his concubine, sent back to Africa with their son. Jostein Gardner's *Vita Brevis* captures popular sentiment well, in the story of an imaginary letter sent by the discarded lover to her man.[41]

The parting was undoubtedly a deeply painful event for both of them. Augustine describes his heart being cut and wounded, and leaving a trail of blood.[42] However, in the culture of the day, Augustine's action would not have been regarded as morally deplorable—unless he had been a baptized, Catholic Christian, which at the time he was not. By the standards of decent Christian behaviour Augustine was clearly wrong. But Augustine was a pagan. And so our criticism of Augustine and Monica's action must be a criticism of Roman culture as a whole, not of this particular mother and son.

Augustine's fiancée was only aged 10 or 11, and, according to Roman law, marriage would have to wait until she was at least 12. Therefore, in the meantime, and in order to satisfy what he describes as his 'insatiable sexual desire,' Augustine took a short-term mistress.

The planned marriage never took place. Famously, Augustine at age 32 underwent a conversion experience in a garden in Milan. He heard a child's voice chanting 'Pick up and read, pick up and read.' He picked up a Bible, opened it and read from Romans 13, 'Not in riots and drunken parties, not in eroticism and indecencies, not in strife and rivalry, but put on the Lord Jesus Christ and make no provision for the flesh in its lusts.' Augustine experienced this as a decisive word from God. All his anxieties lifted and his heart was filled with peace. He simultaneously embraced Christ, gave up his secular ambitions and took a vow of chastity.

It is fascinating to wonder what made Augustine equate turning to Christ with turning away from married life. Partly, no doubt, it was regret at the loss of a woman whom he genuinely loved in favour of a much younger girl who brought a dowry and the right connections. Partly it was the influence of his Platonic (in both senses) male friends, who were frankly unenthusiastic about sex and marriage. And partly it was Augustine's deep admiration for the life of St Anthony and the celibate ideal. On several fronts, Augustine was simply part of a religious (and philosophical) culture which gave low value to sex. He undoubtedly experienced his decision for celibacy as liberation—freedom from the chains of sexual desire and from the social responsibilities of marriage, and freedom to attain to God.

Augustine's Teaching on Sex

Augustine's views of sex changed and developed during his Christian career. They are well illustrated by his developing exegesis of the early chapters of Genesis. As a young Christian, Augustine was disdainful of sex as a distraction from the pursuit of godly wisdom. Thus in his early work, *On Genesis Against the Manichees,* he supposed that there was no sexual reproduction in the Garden of Eden. In the perfect world there are no sexual relations. Sex was given by God, after the Fall, as a remedy for lost immortality.

As his hold on the Christian Scriptures strengthened and matured,[43] Augustine was able to offer a slightly more positive valuation of sex. Thus in his *Literal Commentary on Genesis* he allowed (against the weight of such luminaries as Ambrose, Jerome and Gregory of Nyssa) that there was indeed sexual reproduction in the pre-Fall Garden of Eden. To be sure, he argued against Jovinian (a dangerous radical who thought that all baptized Christians were equal irrespective of marital status!) and with firm biblical grounding in 1 Cor 7.38, that whilst marriage is good, virginity is better. But against the appallingly ascetic Jerome (who thought that Christian marriage could only be a source of regret!) Augustine insisted that marriage is good, and that sex for the purposes of having children is good. Sex divorced from the intent of children was sinful, however, since it pandered to lust ('concupiscence'). Looking back on his own sexual history, Augustine regarded his sexual relationships with women as regrettable and sinful, since they were divorced from marriage and intention to have children. Overall, the mature Augustine thought that sex is a good when directed aright in the service of procreation within marriage, but that it easily becomes diverted into the evil of concupiscence.

Augustine's 'mature' position on marriage has been deeply influential. It lies behind the threefold goods of marriage set out in the Anglican BCP, ASB and *Common Worship*. It is quoted and embodied in Roman Catholic teaching. And, more questionably, it lies behind official Catholic opposition to contraception.

But it is in his later writings that we run into the most problematic aspects of Augustine's teaching. The late Augustine was sure that there was sex in the Garden of Eden. But he now hit on the idea that the effect of the Fall was linked quite directly with a dismal change in human (and specifically male) sexuality. He supposed that before the Fall sexual desire was perfectly ordered under the control of the will, whereas after the Fall, Adam's punishment was to have sexual desire severed from the will. Augustine spares no detail in his sermons to the faithful in explaining how male sexual desire is present when it is not wanted, but fails to rise to the occasion when it is needed. The penalty for Adam's sin was located precisely in the uncontrollable stirring of the genitals. This became the focus in Augustine's writing for the tension between the rational will and the appetites of the flesh. The 'disorder' in sex became the potent symbol of human sin and rebellion against the perfect ordering of the love of God.

The 'disorder' in sex became the potent symbol of human sin and rebellion against the perfect ordering of the love of God

This issue increasingly moved to the centre of one of Augustine's most famous disputes—his controversy with the Pelagians. The Pelagians took a more optimistic view of human nature than Augustine. They found it offensive to suppose that human nature was not basically and intrinsically good, and that human beings have considerable capacity for self-improvement. Augustine was more pessimistic, arguing that without divine grace we are captives of sin. Later Western theology has judged Augustine correct on this issue. However, Augustine's mistake was to hitch (male) sexuality to the issue. And the elderly Augustine became increasingly bad-tempered as he was pushed into a corner here by Julian of Eclanum, the brightest of Augustine's Pelagian opponents, who defended the goodness of sexual desire as we experience it.

Implications for Christian Spirituality
What are the implications of all this for our spirituality today?

- Augustine shared with pretty well all other patristic writers an inability to integrate sexual desire with feelings of love and affection for the beloved. Augustine had some very positive insights concerning the goodness of marriage and the value of friendship between husband and wife. Correcting Augustine's mistakes will mean properly integrating sexual desire within this model of marital companionship and friendship—as *Common Worship* has tried to do. A proper attentiveness to female sexuality is helpful. Moreover, feminist prayers (for example, Janet Morley's *All Desires Known*[44]) provide a contrast and corrective to Augustinian spirituality here.

- Patristic admiration for celibacy derived from a very different social and cultural context from our own. The Roman world of Anthony and Augustine is not our world. Justifications for celibacy today need to be defended within our own social—and indeed psychological—climate. And yet the call to celibacy can be a real challenge to our own sexually preoccupied age. Celibate orders of lay people as well as celibate priests have a long tradition within Christian history and may still have a prophetic role to play in our own culture. And we should reckon with, for example, the immense good done by a generation of women missionaries who sacrificed the opportunity for marriage and family life in order to serve needy human beings in Africa and Asia.

- Isolating the nature of Augustine's errors about sex is important. They are linked to definite theological, philosophical and cultural perspectives. And they are derived partly from the limitations of 5th-century knowledge of our hormonal response systems. They are not a sign that he was 'screwed-up' or 'repressed'! Apart from the abundant evidence that Augustine was a lusty fellow who enjoyed sexual relations with women, it simply does not make sense to use a term that belongs firmly in a post-Freudian language world to describe someone who lived in 5th-century North Africa.

- Whilst Augustine clearly got at least one key aspect of human sexuality wrong, this does not invalidate the whole of his teaching about sex. The comment of the distinguished Augustinian scholar Gerald Bonner is worth pondering:

> His understanding of the deeper issues of sexuality was infinitely more profound than that of the optimistic Julian, and it is difficult to see how any observer, still clinging, however feebly, to traditional Christian values, can fail to be persuaded, with Augustine, that there is some deep disorder in the sexual instinct, as it exists at present in the great majority of the human race.[45]

> For all that we rightly want to affirm the goodness of sexual desire, the reality is that the sex drive very easily goes astray and is the source of much sorrow and suffering.

3. Augustine and Women[46]

There have been attempts to portray Augustine's attitude to women as owing almost everything to his own experiences of love, grief and loss and the assumptions of a patriarchal Graeco-Roman culture, and owing almost nothing to the gospel of Jesus Christ.[47] I think this is mistaken. Augustine's views on the status of women, and his relations with women, are complicated and need to be unpacked rather carefully.

His Pastoral Reserve
Possidius, the biographer of Augustine, describes the saint's dealings with women like this:

> No woman ever lived in his house, or stayed there, not even his own sister…It was the same with his brother's daughters…He used to say that even though no suspicion of evil could arise from his sister or his nieces stopping with him, *they* would have to have other women attending on them and staying with them, and other women again would be coming to see them from outside, and all this might give scandal or prove a temptation to the weak…Even when women asked to interview him, or just to pay their respects, they might never come into his room unless there were clergy there as witnesses. He would never talk to them alone even if the matter were strictly private.[48]

Was this due to demons lurking in Augustine's unconscious, his fear of women or an inability to form normal heterosexual relationships? No, there was surely a much more practical reason for his scrupulosity! Augustine knew from personal experience what defamation of character might mean. A rumour that he had sent love-charms to a married woman delayed his consecration as bishop, and this accusation was rehearsed later in his career by his Donatist opponents. Moreover, he had seen the effect of accusations of impropriety on other clergy. In this light, Augustine was careful to exercise a high level of prudence in face-to-face dealings with women.

By contrast, the evidence shows that Augustine related easily and naturally to women in his written communication. In a letter to the religious Sapida, we hear of him tenderly accepting the gift of a tunic from a girl who had made it for her brother who had sadly died.[49] Or again, he writes to Florentina, offering to assist her with her studies after receiving a request from her parents—the girl herself being too timid to approach the great man. His correspondents included a number of influential upper class religious ladies. Augustine, in his letters to such women, treated his correspondents as intellectual equals, and never shrank from theological exposition at the highest level because of the sex of the recipient.

Subordination and Equivalence

Patristic thinking on the question of the status of women frequently got stuck on 1 Corinthians 11.7—'A man ought not to cover his head since he is the image and glory of God, but the woman is the glory of man.' For most patristic exegetes, this verse quite straightforwardly gave biblical authority to the subordination of women that was, in any case, the cultural norm. Whilst his approach would not satisfy contemporary sensibilities, Augustine is the first author who directly confronts 1 Cor 11.7 by affirming that women too are created in God's image.

Augustine theorises that both men and women are made in the image of God as human (*homo*). However, women are not made in the image of God specifically as women (*femina*). Women and men are thus equal in the order of grace, but women are subordinate to men in the order of nature. Both male and female bodies are willed by God. Augustine specifically rejects the idea that crops up elsewhere in the Christian tradition (and in Roman culture) that women are 'failed men.' As moral and rational agents, women and men are equal, but in their bodily nature women are the weaker sex.

He specifically rejects the idea that women are 'failed men'

Thus, in his analysis of Genesis 2, Augustine notoriously argues that God created woman in order that she might help man through the bearing of children. Augustine's Adam is created in his own right as a God-like exemplary human being, whereas Eve is derived from Adam and therefore subordinate (the order of nature). By contrast, in the last book of *City of God*, Augustine exalts the female body. Women will certainly be resurrected as women. In the world to come their bodies will not excite the lust of men—as there will be no conjugal relations in that life—but will arouse the praises of God. Although Augustine does not actually say so, it seems reasonable to suppose that the result of his analysis is that in the age to come women as women will be equal with men as men (the order of grace).

It would be anachronistic to expect from Augustine an understanding of gender relations appropriate to the 20th or 21st century. Nonetheless, Augustine wrestled hard with these issues and unquestionably took the dignity of women seriously. The Augustinian scholar Kari Børresen provocatively invites us to think of Augustine as a 'patristic feminist' who pushed the equivalence of women and men as far as he could, but was ultimately constrained by an unmistakeably subordinationist St Paul![50]

His Masculinism

What is perhaps more disappointing in Augustine is his apparent lack of appreciation and analysis of femininity. Augustine enjoyed the company of a concubine for 15 years. He had the highest regard for his mother Monica. And he corresponded with higher class religious women as intellectual equals. There is no question that Augustine greatly enjoyed the company of male friends. He offered more penetrating insights on friendship than any other patristic author. Yet Augustine's writings lack any analysis of the non-sexual pleasures and benefits of relationships with women.

There is, in Augustine's character, a sense of Roman toughness and philosophical Stoicism which did not naturally exalt the softer, feminine aspects of human nature. His definite needs for companionship and sympathy were met by men. He was the kind of man who today might have enjoyed the comradeship of the army, or a few decades ago might have inhabited a single sex Oxbridge college.

Moreover, we need to take seriously John Burnaby's comment that 'nearly all that Augustine wrote after his seventieth year is the work of a man whose energy has burnt itself out and whose love has grown cold.'[51] Without being excessively psychoanalytical, it is worth pondering what the hardness revealed in his late works reveals about the true character of the man, even in his younger days. After the dismissal of his concubine, Augustine lacked 'the love of a good woman.' Indeed, his profession of celibacy made this impossible. But if he had been able to sustain even an intimate platonic relationship with women friends, this might have had a profoundly humanizing effect on him that could have significantly nuanced the spiritual legacy with which he endowed later ages.

8 A Contemporary Outworking of Augustinian Spirituality

Having critiqued some of the more problematic aspects of Augustine's work, I now want to be more positive and show one important example of how an Augustinian spirituality can still offer real benefit.

Alcoholics Anonymous is explicitly not a religious society. However, its publications are infused with a certain sense of spirituality, and Christians who have attended an AA meeting (as member or as visitor) cannot but be struck by the quasi-religious nature of the gatherings. I do not imagine that the Americans Bill W and Dr Bob, who founded AA in the 1930s, ever read Augustine directly, but they were influenced by the Christian culture of their day, and the nature of AA spirituality has a surprisingly Augustinian character.

At the heart of AA are 'The Twelve Steps,' which form a kind of spiritual path to healing. These correlate to some extent with the Augustinian path to spiritual wholeness, as follows.

> *Step 1:* 'We admitted we were powerless over alcohol—that our lives had become unmanageable.' This corresponds with the fallen state of humanity according to Augustine. Something that was good in its proper place (alcohol) has, by over-indulgence, gained mastery over us, and displaced God from his rightful place as the object of our highest desires. We are slaves to our sinful desires and as a result our lives have become chronically disordered. The first step in healing is for the person to become aware that he/she is sick.
>
> *Step 2:* 'We came to believe that a Power greater than ourselves could restore us to sanity.' Here the addict realizes his/her basic impotence in the face of disordered desire and the need for a Stronger One to help.
>
> *Step 3:* 'We made a decision to turn our will and our lives over to the care of God *as we understood him*.' The addict realizes the weakness of the will and asks for God's grace to re-orientate his/her life. (Of course, in AA's non-confessional terms, the identity of 'God' is left open.)

Step 4: 'We made a searching and fearless moral inventory of ourselves.'

Step 5: 'We admitted to God, to ourselves and to another human being the exact nature of our wrongs.' Here the addict begins the path of self-knowledge, which is linked (as in Augustine) to the knowledge of God and his knowledge of us. The path to restoration involves fellowship with other AA friends. Likewise, Augustine felt that the Christian spiritual path could only properly be lived in community with fellow Christians.

Step 6: 'We were entirely ready to have God remove all these defects of character.' *Step 7:* 'We humbly asked him to remove our shortcomings.' These two steps correspond to the Augustinian path by which the soul is gradually and painfully made new through the elimination or control of sinful desire.

Steps 8 and *9* refer to reparations that are to be made to those harmed by the addict's behaviour, and *Step 10* re-inforces the commitment to self-examination.

Step 11: 'We sought through prayer and meditation to improve our conscious contact with God, *as we understood him*, praying only for knowledge of his will for us, and the power to carry that out.' In this step, the addict is encouraged to spend more time in the presence of God. Augustine talks about 'delighting in God'—though this would be a little too confessional for AA. Nonetheless, the intention is that the addict's desires and actions will be reshaped through spiritual contact with God.

Step 12: 'Having had a spiritual awakening as the result of these steps, we tried to carry this message to alcoholics, and to practice these principles in our affairs.' Having been substantially healed from errant desire, the person continues to practise and strengthen their new habits and shares the good news of this transformation with others.

AA estimates that some two million people have achieved sobriety through its programme and fellowship. So this form of spirituality quite definitely works, at least for a significant number of addicts. AA is specifically set up to help those who suffer from addiction to alcohol. But the principles would seem to apply to other addictions as well, from drug-taking, through addiction to pornography, to the everyday character weaknesses and compulsions which are a feature of much human—and church—life. In this sense, the 12 Steps could be understood as a specific application of a more general Augustinian spiritual rule of life.

The level of openness and sharing at an AA meeting is striking. Few churches that I have attended have aspired to similar levels of honesty and confidentiality. In this respect, AA comes closer to the demanding form of community life envisaged by Augustine than many church fellowships. It should not be surprising, then, that real character change and spiritual growth can be achieved through AA, whilst such growth is not always very evident in the life of a good number of those who regularly attend our churches. It is one thing to encounter Augustine as a quaint example of patristic spirituality. It is altogether more demanding to imagine and to create forms of church life which embody an Augustinian spirituality for own day.

9

Conclusion

How do you go deeper into Augustinian spirituality?

The simple answer is that Augustinian spirituality is the language of the official liturgy of the Western Reformed church. It is the default option left when we are not following a contemporary variant, such as Celtic, feminist, or New Age spirituality. Within the Anglican church, the Collects and General Confession of the Book of Common Prayer are notably Augustinian (and may be compared with the more humanistic revisions offered in the ASB).

Augustine's Rule[52]—the oldest monastic rule in the West—is an accessible next step. Augustine envisages communities founded on love, in the pattern of the early Jerusalem church of Acts 4. In our age, so dominated by individualism and inequality, this makes challenging reading.

And if your appetite has been whetted, information about further resources can be found on the Grove website www.grovebooks.co.uk under Online Resources.

Augustine was a theological and spiritual giant. Western Christianity owes more to him than anyone else except St Paul. It is perhaps because of the sheer range, depth and complexity of his thought that many Christians know little about this founding Father of the faith. If I have succeeded in dispelling some caricatures, and tempted a few people to want to spend more time in the company of a great saint, then this little work will have been worthwhile.

Notes

1   Website for the British Association for Counselling and Psychotherapy www.bacp.co.uk

2   Jennifer Cunningham quoted in Frank Furedi, *Therapy Culture* (London: Routledge, 2004) p 10.

3   Modern day Annaba on the coast of Algeria.

4   See, for example, Charles Taylor, *Sources of the Self: The Making of the Modern Identity* (Cambridge: CUP, 1989) Chapter 7.

5   See 'The Spirituality of St Augustine and its influence on Western Mysticism' in Gerald Bonner, *God's Decree and Man's Destiny* (Great Yarmouth: Variorum, 1987) pp 143-162.

6   See W Pannenberg, *Systematic Theology Vol II* (Edinburgh: T&T Clarke, 1991) pp 231-265 'sin and original sin.' Contrast, for example, some standard textbooks like A and R Hanson, *Reasonable Belief* (Oxford: OUP, 1981) and Daniel Migliore, *Faith Seeking Understanding* (Grand Rapids: Eerdmans, 1991).

7   Carolinne White, *Christian Friendship in the Fourth Century* (Cambridge: CUP, 1992) p 218.

8   Augustine: *Commentary on John's Gospel* 17.8; *de Trinitate* VIII.8.

9   See James Wetzel, *Augustine and the Limits of Virtue* (Cambridge: CUP, 1992).

10 See further W S Babcock 'Augustine and the Spirituality of Desire' in *Journal of Augustinian Studies Vol 25* (Villanova, 1994) pp 179-199.

11 Rumours to the contrary are without proper foundation. See, for example, Carol Harrison, *Augustine: Christian Truth and Fractured Humanity* (Oxford: OUP, 2000) pp 7-10.

12 Augustine, *Commentary on the First Epistle of John* (New York: CLC Nicene and Post-Nicene Fathers Vol VII ed Schaff, 1888) 4.6.

13 Augustine, *Confessions* III.1, trans F J Sheed (Cambridge: Hackett, 1993).

14 French speakers can read a thorough analysis of this passage in Isabelle Bochet, *Saint Augustin et le désir de Dieu* (Paris: Etudes Augustiniennes, 1982).

15 *Confessions* VIII.5.

16 *Confessions* I.1.

17 *Confessions* X.6. *cf* Romans 1.20.

18 Compare the ascent of *eros* described by Socrates in Plato's *Symposium* (London: Penguin, 1951) p 92f.

19 *Confessions* VII.17.

20 Augustine, *To Simplician—on Various Questions*, English Translation. (London: SCM, 1953) Question 2.21. Augustine, *De Spiritu et Littera*, English Translation (New York: CLC, 1887) NPNF Vol V, Section 3.5.

21 Augustine, *To Simplician, I* question 2.21.

22 *de Trinitate*, 1.5, 9.1 and 15.2.

23 Augustine, *Homilies on the First Epistle of John* 2.10.

24 Augustine, *Homilies on the First Epistle of John* 4.6.

25 *de Trinitate*,14.23.

26 Of course, Augustine did not have access to our modern knowledge of mental illness. In our time, we need to ask what the journey into wholeness means for someone whose *mind* suffers from progressive degradation. See, for example, James Saunders, *Dementia: Pastoral Theology and Pastoral Care* (Grove Pastoral booklet, P 89).

27 Notwithstanding that the general argument and originality of *de Trinitate* lies in its preference for a trinitarian over a Christic *imago Dei*.

28 *de Trinitate* XIV.23.

29 *de Trinitate* XIV.23.

30 *de Trinitate* XIV.25.

31 *City of God* XIV.9.

32 Peter Brown, *Augustine of Hippo* (London: Faber and Faber, 1967) p 170.

33 *City of God* IV.8 and 9.

34 Daniel Goleman, *Emotional Intelligence* (London: Bloomsbury, 1996).

35 *City of God* XIV.9.

36 'On the Life of Plotinus and the Arrangement of his work' in Introduction to the *Enneads*.

37 John Burnaby, *Amor Dei* (London, 1938) p 115. This is seen, for example, in his wariness about the power of sacred music. *Confessions* X.23.

38 Peter Brown, *The Body and Society: Men, Women and Sexual Renunciation in Early Christianity* (London: Faber and Faber, 1990).

39 Brown, p 21ff.

40 *Confessions* VI.15. Manicheeism was a Gnostic sect that held matter to be evil. 'Auditors,' as second class members, were not bound by the celibacy and asceticism required of the first class 'Elect.'

41 Jostein Gardener, *Vita Brevis: A Letter to St Augustine* (London: Phoenix, 1997)—though note that this book seems in part a pretext to indulge in anti-Catholic polemic by way of an imaginary construction of Augustine as a disturbed and violent misogynist.

42 *Confessions* VI.15.

43 The extent to which Neo-platonism retained its hold on Augustine throughout his career has been debated for the last hundred years, and there is a vast literature on the subject.

44 Janet Morley, *All Desires Known* (London: SPCK, 1994).

45 'Libido and Concupiscentia in St Augustine' in Gerald Bonner, *God's Decree and Man's Destiny* (London: Variorum, 1987) p 311.

46 A very balanced treatment is given in Gerald Bonner 'Augustine's Attitude to Women and Amicitia' Cornelius Mayer and Karl Heinz Chelius *Sonderdruck aus Homo Spiritalis* (Wurzburg: Augustinius-Verlag, 1987), pp 259-275, to which I am indebted in this section.

47 See, for example, Kim Power, *Veiled Desire: Augustine on Women* (Continuum: New York, 1996).

48 Possidius, *Vita Augustini* 26:1-3. (London: The Western Fathers, 1954).

49 Augustine, *Letter 263*.

50 Kari Børresen, *Subordination and equivalence: the nature and role of women in Augustine and Thomas Aquinas.* (Washington: University Press of America, 1981).

51 Burnaby, *Amor Dei* (London, 1938) p 231.

52 *The Rule of St Augustine* (London: DLT, 1984).